Poundstock Gildhouse

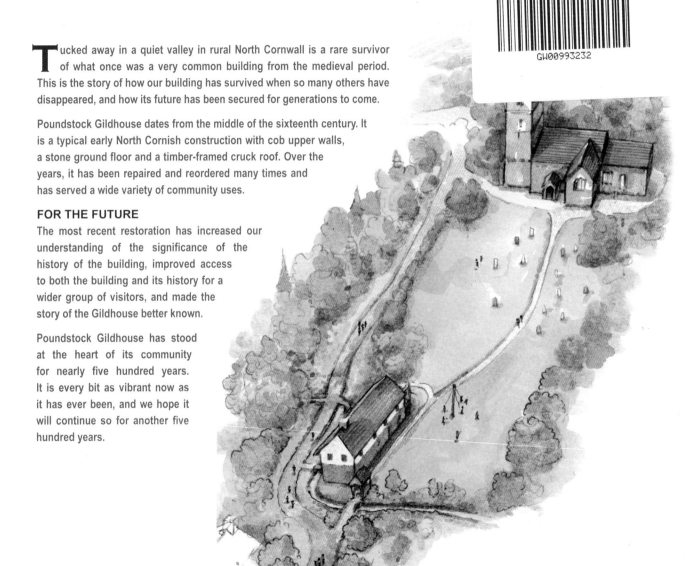

Tucked away in a quiet valley in rural North Cornwall is a rare survivor of what once was a very common building from the medieval period. This is the story of how our building has survived when so many others have disappeared, and how its future has been secured for generations to come.

Poundstock Gildhouse dates from the middle of the sixteenth century. It is a typical early North Cornish construction with cob upper walls, a stone ground floor and a timber-framed cruck roof. Over the years, it has been repaired and reordered many times and has served a wide variety of community uses.

FOR THE FUTURE

The most recent restoration has increased our understanding of the significance of the history of the building, improved access to both the building and its history for a wider group of visitors, and made the story of the Gildhouse better known.

Poundstock Gildhouse has stood at the heart of its community for nearly five hundred years. It is every bit as vibrant now as it has ever been, and we hope it will continue so for another five hundred years.

1066	1086	1282	1337	1357	1387	1431
River Tamar becomes Cornwall's border	Poundstock in Domesday Book	Archbishop visits Poundstock	Duchy of Cornwall established	William Penfound hacked to death	Geoffrey Chaucer *Canterbury Tales*	Jeanne d'Arc burned as witch

The 1500s

Why was the Gildhouse built?

From medieval times the church was the heart of the village and most of village life revolved around it. Apart from the religious aspect, villagers were expected to raise funds to support the poor and to maintain the church building and its many altars. Even in tiny churches there would have been several altars dedicated to different saints including the Virgin Mary. Separate groups, or gilds (not the same as craft guilds), would look after each one, paying for candles and maintenance; for instance, it would usually be the young women of the parish who cared for the altar to the Virgin Mary. At Poundstock, there may well have been an altar to 'the Sunday Christ', who appears in one of the wall paintings as an admonition to villagers not to work on the Sabbath. Money was raised in two ways. The church would own a flock of sheep, and each gild would look after a part of it, with the money from the wool going towards church and altar upkeep. Second, and very important to the social life of the community, money was raised by feasts, known as church ales.

MERRYMAKING

The church gilds would band together to organise an ale, or maybe the churchwardens would call everyone together. These ales would have taken place within the body of the church unless another suitable building was available. Ales were held on all the main feast days of the church year, such as Christmas, Easter and Whitsun as well as the church saint's day. Whitsun was the biggest and longest, with the feasting and merrymaking going on for a whole week. But ales weren't only linked with church festivals: brides' ales were popular events, similar to wedding receptions, and the young men even organised the Tudor equivalent of stag nights. In 1534 Henry VIII made himself head of the Church of England. He was unhappy with the secular use of the church buildings and he let it be known that he did not approve of feasts and markets being held there. Many progressive parishes in and around London had already built 'church houses' for cooking and feasting. Places like Poundstock that had no church house urgently needed to build one.

1431	1470s	1485	1492	1497	1508	1509
Henry VI crowned King of France	Piracy rife along Cornish coast	Henry VII crowned King	Columbus discovers Americas	Cornish uprising against taxation	'Charter of Pardon'	Henry VIII crowned King

HIGH TIMES FOR TUDORS

Despite having contributed to the feast, each villager would pay a penny or tuppence to attend, and the churchwardens, who managed the church accounts and were responsible for the upkeep of the building, would use this money for the maintenance of the church. Besides eating and drinking, there would be dancing and sometimes the rare treat of travelling entertainers. Life was tough in Tudor times and this was one of the few times when people could really let their hair down and enjoy themselves.

THE WHITSUN ALE

Whitsun celebrates the ascension of Jesus into heaven and the coming of the Holy Spirit to the disciples. It takes place fifty days after Easter, in the spring, at a time when for the Tudor farmer ploughing and seed-sowing would have been completed and there was a lull in the farming year. Following church services on Whit Sunday, there would be a week of local celebrations, with each village holding its ale and sharing it with its neighbours, providing an ideal opportunity for young and old to get together. Many a marriage probably resulted from a meeting at a church ale.

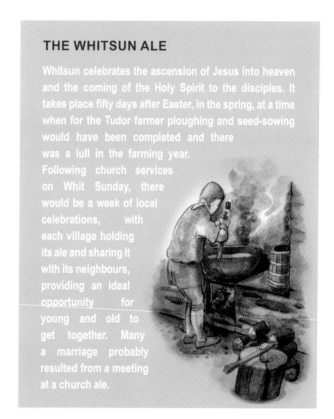

1512	1513	1517	1520	1534	1535	1535
Death of Thomasine Bonaventure	Battle of Flodden English beat Scots	Martin Luther posts '95 theses'	Gunnislake bridge built	Church of England established	Thomas More executed	King Henry VIII excommunicated

1540-1550

A time of turmoil...

*P*oundstock's Gildhouse was one of the last church houses to be built. It began its life during a time of unrest for the church and turmoil throughout the country. It is thought that building work began soon after the Reformation, in the early 1540s, and was probably not finished until about ten years later, during the reign of the boy king Edward VI. Edward was a staunch Protestant and keen to alter many of the old ways. Many, especially in Cornwall, were unhappy with all the changes and some took up arms to express their discontent. Church services had always been in Latin, but Edward decreed that they should now be in English.

REBELLION

The Cornish, not all of whom spoke English, did not want this. Nor did they want to lose the statues, relics and other Catholic artefacts of the church which were now under threat. In 1549 there was outright rebellion and several battles were fought in the South West. Poundstock's vicar, Simon Morton, was one of the leaders of what became known as the Prayer Book Rebellion. Following promises of sympathetic support from young King Edward the rebel forces disbanded, but subsequently the ringleaders were rounded up and executed. For his trouble, Morton was hanged, drawn and quartered in nearby Stratton. So Poundstock

1536	1536	1536 - 1539	1539 - 1545	1540	1540	1544
Anne Boleyn executed	Act of Union joins England and Wales	Destruction of 560 monasteries	Fortifications built along south coast	Gildhouse building underway	Thomas Cromwell executed	Henry VIII's troops occupy Boulogne

lost its vicar and its old way of worship. The parish must have reflected much of the turmoil of the wider area, but somehow, despite all the upheaval, work continued on the new church house.

NATIONAL NOTORIETY

In their Demands to the King, the Western Rebels wrote:

'We wyll have our olde service in Latten, not in Englysh, as it was before, and so we the Cornyshe men (whereof certen of us understand no Englysh), utterly refuse thys newe Englyshe.'

Thanks to Simon Morton, little Poundstock became notorious in London for a while. There was even a ballad written about it:

The vicar of Poundstock with his congregation Commanded them stick to their idolatry; They had much provision and great preparation, Yet God hath given our king victory.

1545	1547	1548	1549	1549
Mary Rose sinks	Edward VI crowned King	Church ales outlawed	First Book of Common Prayer	Prayer Book Rebellion

When and how was it built?

*T*here are no documents surviving from this time to tell us exactly when Poundstock Gildhouse was built, but there are clues in the large oak beams that are in the building. Trees add a ring every year while growing; these vary in size according to the climate, and the patterns created are used by dendrochronologists to date wood. In the Gildhouse several beams still have their rings, and dating shows that one tree was cut down in 1543, probably a couple of years after building work began (they used green oak in those days). Experts think the Gildhouse was probably built between 1540 and 1558 – the mid-Tudor period.

A BUILDING OF STATUS

There is no evidence of when it was completed, but it is thought this would have been before Elizabeth I came to the throne in 1558. The reason such a small building took so long to complete was probably that it was done on a seasonal basis, when the local workmen had time and the lords of the manors could provide the labourers, the materials and the funding. It was probably the Penfounds and the Trebarfoots, local gentry of the time and great rivals, who provided most of this. The Gildhouse was erected within the curtilage of the church, between the churchyard and the stream, on land that probably belonged to the rector. In fact, it may be that bones from earlier graves had to be moved out of the way.

A hive of industry was created, with labourers, masons and carpenters toiling to erect an important new building. Expense was not spared and a relatively large building was erected, over 60 feet long and 20 feet wide, with a ten-bay roof. This was no common shed but a high-status building, as shown by the carved oak ogee windows and the dressed floor joists. In Tudor times all materials would

1550	1553	1553	1555	1558	1558	1567
Roger Harward Poundstock vicar	Mary I 'Bloody Mary' begins 5 yr reign.	Mary I allows church ales	Richard Carew born at Antony	Calais retaken by French	Elizabeth I Queen begins 45 yr reign	Spanish land at Penryn

be sourced locally, which meant wood felled nearby, stones collected from the beach, sandstone and slate dug from local quarries, and cob materials collected from the surrounding fields. Large beach boulders created the foundations and the ground floor was built of sandstone probably quarried nearby. The floor was trampled earth, hard like concrete. Masons built the stone walls up to the first-floor level, working from wooden platforms called hurdles. They also built an outside staircase at the north end and a large chimney and fireplaces to the south.

THE HEART OF THE PARISH

The downstairs fireplace contained cloam ovens for baking and plenty of space for brewing and cooking. Carpenters made windows, doors, roof and floors (possibly in that order) using wood that probably came from the nearby Millook valley. No one knows for certain whether the original building was thatched or had a slate roof, but the finding of a pottery ridge tile of early date does suggest that the roof was of slate, which at that time would most likely have come from Tintagel. At last, Poundstock had its own church house. The Gildhouse, as it became known (and spelt), was soon the strongly beating heart of the parish.

COB RECIPE

Ingredients:

Soil from the fields
Straw from the farm
Dung and urine from the cows

Method: Take your soil to the cowshed. Add straw. Let the cows in and leave them to do their business. Leave them to trample it to the correct consistency. Apply to walls in layers 4–6 inches thick. Leave to dry and repeat as necessary. Makes a fine strong cob that lasts for hundreds of years.

1570	1585	1585	1585
Francis Drake sets sail to West Indies	Murder plot against Queen Elizabeth I	Start of Anglo Spanish war	Prideaux Place Padstow is begun

The 1500s

A church ale...

Church ales were vital to social life in country parishes and were essential to raising funds for the church and supporting the poor. In Tudor times everyone in the parish, rich or poor, was part of the church and came to enjoy the church ales and the merrymaking that took place. People from nearby parishes were also invited and came to join in the fun, with feasting, dancing, plays, such as the story of St George and the Dragon, or maybe entertainment from jugglers or bear baiting. Young people of the parish aged between 12 and 22 would go to the local landowners to beg the ingredients for the feast: fish and meat for stews, flour for bread and cakes, barley and honey for ale, butter and cheese.

BAKING

They then baked and brewed in the lower-floor kitchen using the big Tudor fireplace, which would have taken up the whole south wall. Gorse would be burned in the cloam ovens in the wall of the fireplace and then the ashes raked out. Bread dough, risen and shaped into loaves, was put in and the door, which was a separate clay structure with a handle, was put in place and sealed with some spare dough. When the seal was cooked, so was the bread inside. These ovens were also used by local housewives on weekdays to bake the family bread as most cottages only had open fires at this date.

BREWING

The small beer brewed for the ales was the usual drink at a time when water was often unsafe to drink. It was brewed in the kitchens on a weekly basis for the whole community, not just for feasts.

1586	1586	1587	1588	1588	1590	1591
Sir Walter Raleigh reveals tobacco	Sir Thomas Harriot introduces potatoes	Mary Queen of Scots executed	Enemy Spaniards land in Mounts Bay	Spanish Armada defeated	Pope Urban VII dies after just 13 days	First performance of Shakespeare

The fermentation process killed harmful bacteria, and the resulting beer contained very little alcohol.

FEASTING

On the feast day itself the young people would serve the rest of the parishioners, who were crammed into the upper feasting hall, furnished with forms and trestle tables. Everyone paid a penny or tuppence to eat the food for which they had provided the ingredients – a tradition that still goes on today!

BREAD PLATE RECIPE

In order to feed everyone with stew and with plates in short supply, Tudors baked bread plates. These not only served as suitable containers but were also edible – bread was one of the staple foods of the day. Even the kitchen workers benefited, as there was no washing up!

To make 6 plates:
4 cups strong flour – from the miller
1 teaspoon salt – evaporated from seawater
1 tablespoon butter – from the farmer's wife
1 tablespoon sugar or honey – from the manor house
1 tablespoon fresh yeast – from the brewer
1 cup of warm water mixed with milk – from the farmer

In a jug mix the sugar with the yeast and add the milk and water. Put in a warm place until the mixture starts to bubble. In a bowl place the flour and the salt then rub in the butter with your fingertips.
Add the bubbling yeast mixture gradually to the flour and mix to a soft dough; more water can be added if needed. Place the dough on a floured board and knead till smooth. Put back in bowl, cover and leave to double in size.
Punch and squeeze the dough a little then divide into six even pieces. Knead a little and shape into a ball. Press firmly with heel of hand into a disc shape and press evenly all round until the size of a saucer.
Prick all over with a fork and place on a baking sheet. Leave to rise again for 20 minutes in a warm place, then cook in a hot oven (200 degrees) for about 10 minutes until golden.

1595	1598	1598	1600	1600	1600	1600
Spanish fleet attack Mousehole	Parliament sends convicts to colonies	Peter Dennis Poundstock vicar	East India Company formed	Britain's population reaches 4 million	Mining at St Agnes 'Polberro Mine'	Survey of Cornwall published

1550-1600 Feasting and fun...

After the feast came the fun, which probably included Maypole dancing, country dancing and maybe even fertility dances akin to the Hobby Hoss dance of Padstow. Occasional entertainment was supplied by travelling troupes of 'Egyptians', or gypsies, who earned a copper or two by juggling, bareback riding and fortune telling. In Whitsun week, people from nearby parishes were also celebrating, and time was spent entertaining or being entertained by the folk of the surrounding villages. It was a chance to catch up on old friendships and make new ones.

POPULAR

We know that about 500 people attended the feasts in the Gildhouse. This surprisingly high number is well documented as Poundstock still has its 1540 muster roll, a list of all able-bodied males between 16 and 60 who could be called on to fight for the monarch if the need arose. In fact, the parish armour was also stored in the Gildhouse and the men would use the longbows and targets to practise their skills after church on Sundays. The Poundstock muster roll has 240 names. Double this number to include females, add more for the elderly and infirm and those under 16, and you get close to the 500 figure.

ALES

Church ales were a feature of parish life for about 200 years. Eventually they acquired a reputation for disorderliness and drunkenness and various attempts were made by different monarchs to stop them, but none succeeded – it took a war to do that.

1603	1605	1629	1642	1643	1646
James I unites England & Scotland	Guy Fawkes Gunpowder Plot	Parliament dissolved	1st English Civil War started	Battle of Stratton	Roundheads reach Bodmin

1649-1660

End of an era...

$\mathcal{T}$he English Civil War between the Royalists and the Puritans and the subsequent rule of Cromwell as Lord Protector had an enormous effect on life in the seventeenth century and consequently on what went on in our Gildhouse. All feasting and fun ceased – even birthdays and Christmas were frowned upon. This Commonwealth period, as it became known, lasted from 1649 to 1660, when, with Charles II, the monarchy was restored; however, feasting with church ales was not.

ALL CHANGE

Things had changed. People had begun to give their money on a Sunday with the church collection and landowners paid their tithes directly to the clergy. Fixed pews had been put into most churches, preventing the use of the building for anything except worship. Social needs had changed, and the bishops asked the parishes to provide schooling and poor housing. The Poor Law decreed that if you became destitute you had to return to your parish of birth, where they had to take care of you.

CHANGE OF USE

Church houses all over the country had lost their role as places for feasting and fun and were used for little more than storage and meetings. They were the obvious choice of building to house schools and poor relief. Poundstock's Gildhouse was no exception.

1648	1649	1649	1652	1652	1660	1660
2nd English Civil War started	King Charles I executed	Commonwealth replaces monarchy	William Greenaway Poundstock vicar	Tea arrives in Britain	Monarchy restored with Charles II	Church revels legal again

1660-1800

Changes...

In the second half of the seventeenth century the Gildhouse underwent a large alteration to become both a school and a poorhouse.

The huge Tudor fireplace was removed and the present chimney stack was built, together with a second one towards the other end of the building. With the resulting fireplaces this created three rooms on the upper floor.

The biggest became a schoolroom, with a fireplace at each end, and the two smaller rooms became poor rooms, each with their own door and fireplace.

CLUES TO THE PAST
A newly created internal staircase led up to the schoolroom from a small vestibule downstairs. Today you can still see where the beam was chamfered to create sufficient headroom.

CHANGE OF USE
Downstairs, in what had been the Tudor kitchen, windows were turned into doorways and a wooden partition was built across the middle; with the new chimney breasts, this created a further four poor rooms.

1665	1689	1721	1723	1738	1757	1776
Great Plague of London	English Bill of Rights	Sir Robert Walpole first PM	Poor Law Act - workhouses	Birth of Methodist movement	Wedgwood Pottery founded	America declares independence

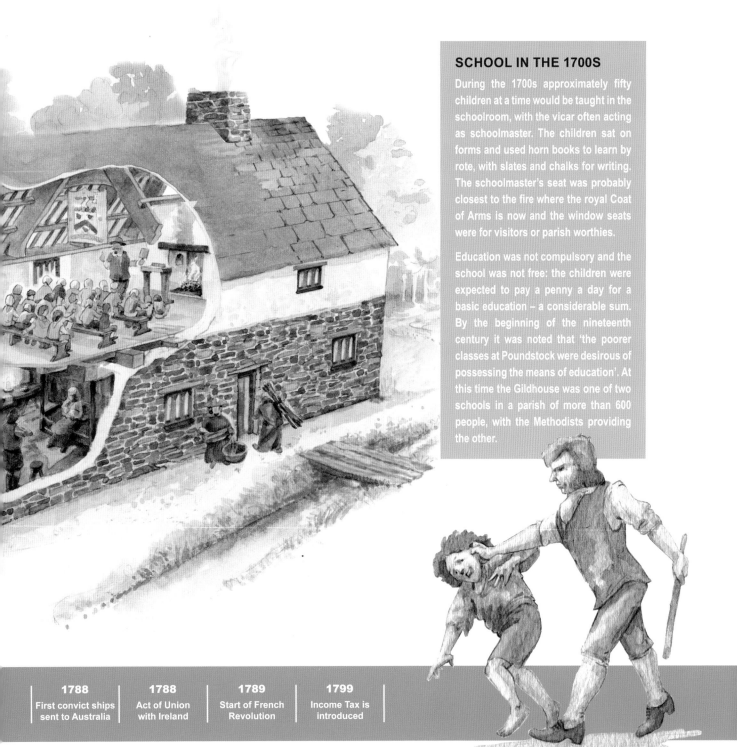

SCHOOL IN THE 1700S

During the 1700s approximately fifty children at a time would be taught in the schoolroom, with the vicar often acting as schoolmaster. The children sat on forms and used horn books to learn by rote, with slates and chalks for writing. The schoolmaster's seat was probably closest to the fire where the royal Coat of Arms is now and the window seats were for visitors or parish worthies.

Education was not compulsory and the school was not free: the children were expected to pay a penny a day for a basic education – a considerable sum. By the beginning of the nineteenth century it was noted that 'the poorer classes at Poundstock were desirous of possessing the means of education'. At this time the Gildhouse was one of two schools in a parish of more than 600 people, with the Methodists providing the other.

1788	1788	1789	1799
First convict ships sent to Australia	Act of Union with Ireland	Start of French Revolution	Income Tax is introduced

1800-1841

The poor and the Dissenters...

We can see the value of literacy in the parish from this time onwards by looking at church registers, where the number of people able to sign their names rather than making a cross increased significantly. Anglican children continued to attend the Gildhouse school, but by the beginning of the 1800s there was an alternative school and numbers were decreasing; the Methodist Church, known as the Dissenters, was growing fast, and the newly built Bangors Chapel near the present A39 also provided education for its children. Consequently, the Gildhouse schoolroom was halved in size, creating a third poor room upstairs.

PROVIDING FOR THE POOR

The Gildhouse now had seven poor rooms available to the destitute or homeless. Applications were made to the Church Council, and if a room was available you would be given it. The type of people in the poorhouse included the old and infirm who were unable to work and so had lost their tied cottages, widows and those who were homeless for a variety of reasons.

Even young families who had no other accommodation would be housed here. They were expected to pay a few shillings a year in rent – if they could afford it.

With seven rooms for the poor, there may have been twenty to thirty people living in the Gildhouse, or even more. Their water came not from the stream but from the well just across the road. What happened to their waste is not known!

1801	1801	1805	1806	1807	1809	1810
Trevithick's steam locomotive	First British census	Nelson wins Battle of Trafalgar	Caerhayes Castle built	Slave trade abolished	First OS mapping of Cornwall	*West Briton* first published

THE POOREST OF THE POOR

Both young and old were given rooms in the poorhouse in the eighteenth and nineteenth centuries. Life was difficult and cramped for those who had fallen on hard times, but each room had its own doorway and fireplace which allowed some independence and dignity.

We have no record of any gardens for the inhabitants and food would often have been scarce. A layer of limpet shells found by the stream suggests that the very poor of the Gildhouse collected shellfish from nearby beaches and relied on them as part of their diet.

1815	1817	1823	1825	1829	1830	1837
Humphry Davy's mine safety lamp	Destitute Penfounds live in Gildhouse	Bude canal completed	Poor Law sets up workhouses	Metropolitan Police founded	Bude Castle built	Victoria becomes Queen

1841-1881

Clues from the census...

In 1841 the first national census was introduced, just as a new vicar of Poundstock, Philip Dayman, took up his post. Dayman was keen to know how many of his parishioners did not attend his church – who were Dissenters (Methodists), in other words – and therefore how this affected his salary.

He made notes on his rights and responsibilities and carried out his own census. Dayman's notes and the national census records show who lived in the poorhouse and which rooms they occupied.

THE STACEY FAMILY

In one of the poorhouse rooms, according to the 1841 census, lived William Stacey, aged 30, an agricultural labourer, born in the county of Cornwall. With him lived his wife Mary, aged 35, and their son Samuel, 5, daughter Mary, 3, and baby Betsy, aged just six months.

The Stacey family were still living in the Gildhouse when the 1851 census was taken. However, the makeup of the family had changed.

Mary, the wife, was still there, along with Betsy, now 11, and three younger children, John, William and Grace.

William, the father, was not recorded, nor were the two older children, Samuel and Mary, who may have gone into service.

Philip Dayman,
Vicar of Poundstock 1841

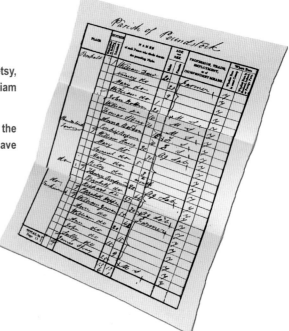

1843	1844	1847	1853 - 1856	1854	1854	1859
Dickens published *A Christmas Carol*	Railway Act forces affordable service	Henry Penfound dies aged 86	The Crimean War	Elizabeth Penfound dies	Charge of the Light Brigade	Brunel's Royal Albert Bridge

18

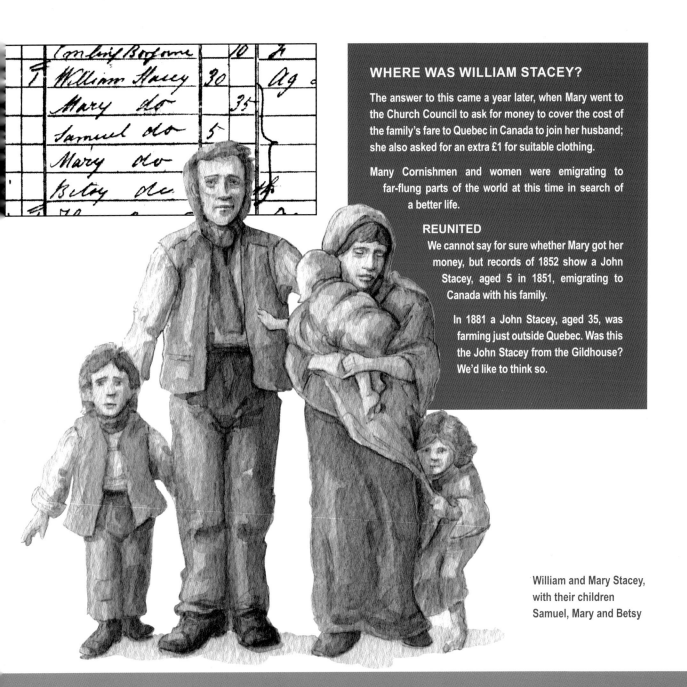

WHERE WAS WILLIAM STACEY?

The answer to this came a year later, when Mary went to the Church Council to ask for money to cover the cost of the family's fare to Quebec in Canada to join her husband; she also asked for an extra £1 for suitable clothing.

Many Cornishmen and women were emigrating to far-flung parts of the world at this time in search of a better life.

REUNITED

We cannot say for sure whether Mary got her money, but records of 1852 show a John Stacey, aged 5 in 1851, emigrating to Canada with his family.

In 1881 a John Stacey, aged 35, was farming just outside Quebec. Was this the John Stacey from the Gildhouse? We'd like to think so.

William and Mary Stacey, with their children Samuel, Mary and Betsy

1860	1861 - 1865	1865	1865	1866	1868	1869
St Day Brickworks begun	American Civil War	Abraham Lincoln assassinated	Slavery in the US is outlawed	Low copper prices cause emigration	Last public hanging	Wolf Rock Light-house completed

1881-1901

From riches to rags...

On the ground floor of the Gildhouse next door to the Stacey family lived Henry Pollexfen Penfound, his wife Elizabeth and their son Richard, who was blind.

Henry was the last direct descendent of the Penfounds of Penfound Manor, the family who had probably been one of the original benefactors of the Gildhouse.

The Penfounds had long since left the manor having lost their fortune, possibly through gambling debts or support given to the ill-fated Jacobite Rebellion.

Penfound Manor
circa 1642

1870	1873	1874	1875	1876	1880	1881
Education Act school for everyone	'Long Depression' stock market crash	Levi Strauss invents 'blue jeans'	Duke of Cornwall sails down the Nile	Alexander Bell invented telephone	Gladstone Prime Minister	First Boer war

Family Coat of Arms

PENFOVND

TEN TO A ROOM

By 1817 these last direct descendants were paupers and were sent back home to Poundstock from Minster parish near Boscastle.

They then had eight children living with them, so ten people had to share one room; the youngest was baby James, aged 1 month.

Given these conditions, it is not surprising that James died in the Gildhouse aged 5 months in 1818.

Henry died in 1847 aged 86 and Elizabeth died in 1854, both in the poorhouse. Richard, the blind son, was moved to Stratton Poorhouse but returned in 1881, living on parish relief.

MOVED TO THE WORKHOUSE

Many other names of paupers survive but their stories are hard to trace.

The last pauper residents were noted in 1891 and by 1901 the building was empty, all inhabitants having been transferred to the dreaded and newly built workhouse in Stratton.

This is the earliest photograph we have of the Gildhouse, and illustrates the awful state of the building. The Gildhouse was now empty and redundant and according to parish records in a 'state of decrepitude'; a drain on the parish who could no longer afford its upkeep. Little wonder that the parish considered demolishing it!

This state of affairs was repeated all over the West Country and it was when many of these buildings ceased to exist. The once beating heart of the parish almost stopped...

State of decay - the Gildhouse before 1907 restoration

1885	1886	1887	1891	1897	1900	1901
Tesla builds radio transmitter / receiver	First free public library in Truro	Sherlock Holmes first published	Last paupers living in Gildhouse	HG Wells published *War of the Worlds*	Anually 550,000 tons china clay extracted	Gildhouse empty

1901-1960 The heart beats again...

By now, the government had taken on responsibility for educating children up to the age of 10 and a new national school had been built up on the main road. The schoolroom was no longer needed and now the poor had gone too, leaving the Gildhouse empty and redundant.

DISREPAIR

This state of affairs was repeated all over the West Country, and it was at this time that many church houses became pubs or private homes or were simply demolished. In Poundstock, the building still stood, but according to parish records was in a 'state of decrepitude', a drain on the parish, which could no longer afford its upkeep. The once beating heart of the parish had almost stopped. Its fate was in the balance.

Covered in ivy, sagging, damp and in poor repair, the building was in danger of falling down. Who took pity on it is not known, but somehow money was found for a major restoration of the Gildhouse in the early years of the twentieth century. By 1907, under the guidance of Exeter architect Edmund Sedding, the building had undergone a complete transformation.

REBIRTH

Sedding's restoration was firmly in sympathy with the building's Tudor origins. He removed most of the post-Tudor additions and restored as many of the Tudor features as he could, replacing only as necessary. The chimney stack at the north end of the building was removed, together with the poorhouse partitions and internal staircase.

View from the church

1901	1902	1904	1905	1905	1907	1910
Marconi transmits transatlantic signal	Camborne and Redruth Tramway	Handbook of the Cornish Language	Gildhouse used again by locals	Einstein publishes $E=MC^2$ equation	Sedding Gildhouse restoration	Truro Cathedral completed

Gildhouse post restoration

The sagging walls were supported with buttresses and ties and roof trusses were replaced where necessary. Downstairs, a parquet floor was laid, doors were removed, windows restored and glass shutters added throughout to let the light in.

MOD CONS

Upstairs in the feasting room, some new floorboards were laid, although the wider Tudor boards still remain at the south end, and old windows were uncovered on each side of the main door. Keeping the south end chimney stack meant that a spanking new kitchen, complete with an up-to-the-minute copper boiler, could be created to bring modernity to what now became the new village hall.

Poundstock post 1911, after restoration

REVIVAL

The building today owes much to Edmund Sedding as it was his vision and thoroughness that restored the Gildhouse to the atmosphere of its Tudor origins. From 1905 onwards it took on a new lease of life, being used for parish festivals, the Sunday school and the Men's Club. The club had books and games and there was a broad settle by the hearth downstairs where village gaffers smoked pipes and discussed local affairs.

By 1945 there was a lecture hall, a library and a committee room, and social events were a regular feature. Whist drives frequently took place, and Full Moon dances were very popular – not for any romantic reason, but because, with no electricity, on dark nights you had to be very careful not to fall into the stream at the front of the building when the dance ended!

1912	1914 - 1918	1921	1929	1931	1932	1937
RMS *Titanic* sinks	The First World War	Dolcoath Copper Mine closes	Wall Street banking crash	Roman Villa at Camborne found	First play at Minack Theatre	Sir Frank Whittle invents jet engine

1960-2000

Coming full circle...

As the twentieth century moved on and society changed, the Gildhouse remained locked in almost a time warp. Very little was done to it except urgent repairs, and those at the least possible cost to the church. Once again it began a slow decline into decrepitude. Towards the end of the century the building still had no permanent heating and was suffering the ravages of fungus, woodworm and storm damage.

Electricity and running water were eventually installed in the 1970s but the building was no longer being used by the community, which now had the attractions of television and had become more mobile with the increase in car ownership. Sitting in a cold damp draughty building with limited conveniences was not an attractive option.

LISTED STATUS
In 1961, English Heritage recognised the rarity of the Gildhouse as one of the few surviving Tudor church houses in the entire region and gave it a Grade 1 listing but did not provide any funding for it.

While this protected the building, it also placed a heavy burden on the small congregation of St Winwaloe's Church, who were responsible for its repair and maintenance within the constraints of the listing.

A LEGACY RECEIVED
They had no experience and next to no funds. The building had become an albatross around the neck of the Parochial Church Council and the future looked bleak.

But once again, fortune stepped in. At the crucial time the church received a legacy from Mrs Marjorie Joyce Hayne of Penfound Manor, and this was to become the catalyst to setting up a committee to redecorate and update the facilities in the Gildhouse in the hope it would be used as a social venue.

Initial site visit 2004

'Witch bottle' in poorhouse

Foundation - beach stones

Items found during works

1939	1939 - 1945	1939	1944	1944	1945	1945
Hollywood releases *Gone with the Wind*	The Second World War	St Ives lifeboat tragedy	Bletchley Park builds 'electronic' computer	Normandy landings depart south coast	Lecture hall and library in Gildhouse	Atomic bombs dropped on Japan

Tired Gildhouse, May 2004

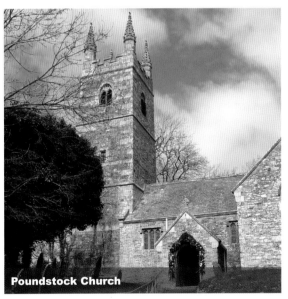
Poundstock Church

THE COAT OF ARMS

Royal Coats of Arms had been displayed in all churches since the time of Henry VIII as a sign of loyalty. Through the intervening centuries, many were changed as royal houses came and went.

Our Coat of Arms, despite appearances, dates from 1638 and the reign of Charles I but was altered in the Hanoverian period to show the arms of George III. It originally hung on the north wall of the church opposite the entrance, but when the medieval wall paintings were discovered in 1901 it was moved into the tower.

However, the damp conditions there were causing the wooden backing to deteriorate and threatening the plasterwork, so in the 1980s it was moved into the Gildhouse for expert restoration.

A stainless steel backing was put on and a four-inch plaster border added for stability. At this point it became clear that the restored coat of arms was now too big to go back the way it had come, and since then it has had pride of place in the feasting hall.

The colours are original and it is possible they may reflect the colours of the hall in Tudor times.

1947	1951	1952
Sound barrier broken	Mebyon Kernow formed	Elizabeth II becomes Queen

2000-2008

The 21st century restoration...

It was soon realised that one small legacy was not going to cover the cost of the structural work needed to repair the Gildhouse. Because of the Grade I listing, English Heritage became involved and a full survey was commissioned. Meanwhile, large lumps of cob had fallen off the walls and some beams were at risk of being compromised by water penetration. It was clear that a major fundraising effort was needed.

FUNDING THE PROJECT

Under the leadership of Tim Dingle, Rev. Rob Dickenson and Rev. Gavin Douglas, funding was obtained from a wide variety of sources. The Heritage Lottery Fund provided an amazing 89 per cent grant, and practical and financial support was generously given by North Cornwall District Council with additional support from charitable trusts and many local people.

Experts were called in to do a thorough study of the history and structure of the building. This included tree-ring dating, documentary analysis, an archaeological survey and, most importantly, full structural surveys.

PEOPLE SKILLS

The challenges posed by the restoration were many, not least the inexperience of the committee to meet those challenges. However, what was lacking in experience was more than made up for in enthusiasm and love for this beautiful old building and a determination to save it.

It was not just getting the required funding to do the job. Finding an architect, surveyors and craftsmen with the appropriate skills was one of the many tasks that had to be undertaken. Heritage builders had to be used, and everything had to be done correctly, with much form filling and meetings under the guidance of English Heritage.

Nothing could be repaired without their permission and oversight. But all these difficulties were overcome, and between 2004 and 2008 a major restoration project was carried out.

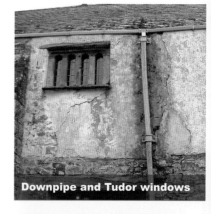

Downpipe and Tudor windows

Limpet shells evidence

1959	1961	1961	1961	1963	1963	1964
Last Cornish beam engine ceases work	Gildhouse receives Grade 1 listing	Tamar road bridge opens	First man in space Yuri Gagarin	J F Kennedy assassinated	Pedestrian precinct begun in St Austell	Penzance to Scilly helicopter starts

26

Windows ready for repair

Master craftsman at work

THE ARCHITECT

Appointing the right architect was the key, and we were fortunate enough to find Jonathan Rhind of Jonathan Rhind Architects Ltd.

One of the highest accolades we can give him is that he became the Sedding of the twenty-first century. His detailed and meticulous restoration has saved and secured the Gildhouse while at the same time keeping its integrity, its heart.

Thank you, Jonathan.

RESTORATION

• Opening up fireplaces

• Repairing all windows and doors

• Taking off all plaster and replastering

• Renewing french drain

• Putting in new kitchen and two toilets

• Roof extened by four layers of slate with more effective guttering to prevent water penitration of walls

• The National Lottery gave an 89% grant and even helped fund the car park and lighting to the Gildhouse through the churchyard

1964	1967	1967	1968	1969	1973	1975
Harold Wilson Prime Minister	*Torrey Canyon* disaster	The Beatles visit Newquay	Martin Luther King assassinated	America lands man on moon	UK joins European Community	Legacy received for restoration

2008...
Bringing the Gildhouse back to life..

Once the fabric of the Gildhouse had been restored and the building was safe for future generations, the biggest challenge was to get the public, and in particular the community, to use the building again. Several generations even within the parish barely knew the building existed, so raising its restored profile was of prime importance.

'Use it or lose it' became the motto as the newly formed committee tried to come up with as many ways to make use of this beautiful unique building as possible. We also had to fulfil our obligations to the Heritage Lottery Fund, whose generous grant of £380,000 made the restoration possible, to make the building available to the wider public and help them understand its cultural and historical importance.

TUDOR DAYS

The Gildhouse has become an exciting, vibrant centre for bringing history to life through a comprehensive hands-on approach to learning for children and adults alike.

As part of the Gildhouse education outreach, they come to be Tudors for a day. Spending half the day as Tudor peasants and half as Tudor aristocracy, dressing up as rich and poor, they take part in activities that went on in the Tudor period in the Gildhouse – baking, brewing, dancing, music-making . . . They absorb a huge amount of historical knowledge and have fun doing it: the best way to learn.

AND MUCH MORE

The committee have organised regular community talks and many groups come to the Gildhouse for a historical tour and talk, often ending with the famous Cornish cream tea. The building is also open to the general public every Wednesday from Easter to October with volunteers on hand to tell the story if needed and to provide a welcome cup of tea; there is no charge.

As for the community, they have responded by hiring the building for a variety of celebrations including wedding receptions, bringing us back full circle to the brides' ales of yore.

1977	1980	1981	1984	1986	1988	1989
Deep space probe Voyager I launched	Sinclair ZX80 DIY home computer	Penlee Lifeboat disaster	First Apple Macintosh PC	David Penhaligon MP dies car accident	Pan Am 103 bombed over Lockerbie	Berlin Wall falls

Tudor Day

MUSIC

Music features quite frequently in the programme and artists have remarked not only on the good acoustics but on the wonderful feeling the Gildhouse has. The committee continues to promote the use of the building in as many ways as possible.

FRIENDS OF THE GILDHOUSE

The Gildhouse now provides a focus for parish activities, just as it has done for 500 years, and we hope it will continue to do so well into the future. But it will always need friends.

If you care about this precious building, please join the Friends of the Gildhouse to help ensure that it continues to survive and thrive.

Visit **www.poundstockgildhouse.co.uk** for full details.

Local meeting place

Craft Fair at the Gildhouse

1989	1991	1991	1991	1992	1994	1998
Martin Potter World Surfing Champion	First windfarm in Cornwall	First Gulf War	World Wide Web invented	Tate Gallery St Ives opens	Channel Tunnel opens	South Crofty Tin Mine closes

Noteworthy

Things to look out for.

One of the most special qualities about the Gildhouse is that you can trace its history through the very fabric of the building. Each period has left its mark if you know what to look for.

Here are just a few.

FROM THE TUDOR PERIOD
• Roof of feasting hall – construction/smoke blackening/blade marks on beams
• Ogee oak windows
• Dressed beams on downstairs joists

FROM THE SEVENTEENTH TO NINETEENTH CENTURIES
• Chimney stack with fireplaces for school and poor rooms and cloam ovens
• Chamfered beam for internal staircase, lower floor
• Witch bottle dated 1720, fireplace, upper floor, a charm against witchcraft

AFTER SEDDING'S RESTORATION
• Traces of doorways below restored lower-floor windows
• External buttresses
• Glass window shutters

Smoke-darkened roof timbers

Site of poorhouse door

Chamfered beam

1907 window shutters

16th century ogee

16th century broad floorboards

2000	2001	2001	2003	2004	2007	2007
Total eclipse seen over Cornwall	The Eden Project opens near St Austell	World Trade Center attacked	Invasion of Iraq	Boscastle flooded	Gildhouse restoration starts	Global financial crisis